DISASTERS AND THE ENVIRONMENT

DROUGHTS and the Environment

by Marcia Amidon Lusted

CAPSTONE PRESS
a capstone imprint

Published by Capstone Press, an imprint of Capstone
1710 Roe Crest Drive, North Mankato, Minnesota 56003
capstonepub.com

Library of Congress Cataloging-in-Publication Data is available on the Library of Congress website.
ISBN: 9798875216947 (hardcover)
ISBN: 9798875216893 (paperback)
ISBN: 9798875216909 (ebook PDF)

Summary: Droughts can cause a lot of damage to the environment. Find out how droughts affect land and animals and how nature can recover from these long periods of dry weather.

Editorial Credits
Editor: Ashley Kuehl; Designer: Dina Her; Media Researcher: Jo Miller; Production Specialist: Tori Abraham

Image Credits
Getty Images: David Gray, 27, 29, Diana Robinson Photography, 17, Ed Ram, 15, iStock/ Cynthia Shirk, 14, Joe Raedle, 13, Jonathan Knowles, 19, Justin Sullivan, 5, Mario Tama, 18, Oli Scarff, 26, Scott Olson, 22; Shutterstock: AlbertoGonzalez, 21, Dark_Side, 16, Dietrich Leppert, cover (top), Everett Collection, 12, Grusho Anna, 8, Jsvideos, 24, montree hanlue, cover (bottom), noer cungkring, 6, PACO COMO, 23, Ramsey Samara, 9, Sergiy Bykhunenko, 20, Sharad Raval, 25, Stanislav71, 11, Tanja Esser, 10, Vector Tradition (cracks), cover and throughout, zombiu26, 7

Printed and bound in China. 006276

TABLE OF CONTENTS

INTRODUCTION
Running Out of Water 4

CHAPTER ONE
A Dry Land 6

CHAPTER TWO
Dry, Cracked Soil 10

CHAPTER THREE
What Happens to Animals 14

CHAPTER FOUR
After a Drought 18

CHAPTER FIVE
Humans and Drought 24

Glossary 30
Read More 31
Internet Sites 31
Index 32
About the Author 32

Words in **bold** are in the glossary.

RUNNING OUT OF WATER

It began in 2021 in California. The spring and summer had been hot. Not enough rain fell. Rivers, lakes, and **reservoirs** were drying up. The dry conditions started forest fires. Tens of millions of people live in California. The state has huge ranches and farms. Everyone needed water. Now there wasn't enough. The Colorado River was running out of water. No one could remember that happening before. Two big reservoirs supply water to California. But both Lake Mead and Lake Powell were less than half full.

FACT

In California, each year from 2016 through 2023 set new records for the warmest year ever. This makes drought worse.

Scientists called it a megadrought. This is a serious drought that lasts a long time. The government was worried about the water supply. The governor of California, Gavin Newsom, said the state was officially in a drought. He announced strict rules about using and saving water. The California megadrought was the worst drought to hit the state in 1,200 years.

The 2021 drought nearly dried out Lake Powell. The lake was running low in June 2021 (top). Parts of it were dry by March 2022 (bottom).

Chapter One

A DRY LAND

What is a drought? And how does it happen? A drought is a long period of time when the weather is much drier than usual. Much less rain or snow falls than is normal for the area. A drought lasts for an entire season. It may even last for months or years. Drought can cause changes to plants, animals, and the environment.

A field affected by drought in Indonesia.

Drought can happen when Earth's water cycle is disrupted. Water **evaporates** from rivers, streams, lakes, and oceans. It rises into the **atmosphere**. A **current** of wind called the **jet stream** moves this moisture around Earth. Sometimes the jet stream is blocked or changes its path. It might stop bringing the clouds that lead to rain.

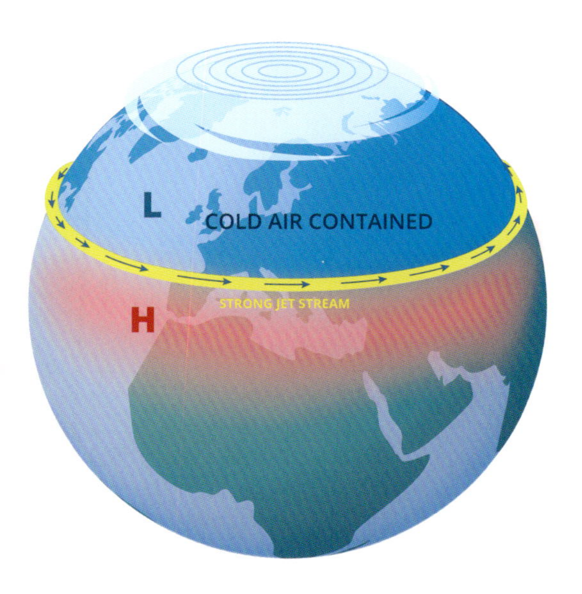

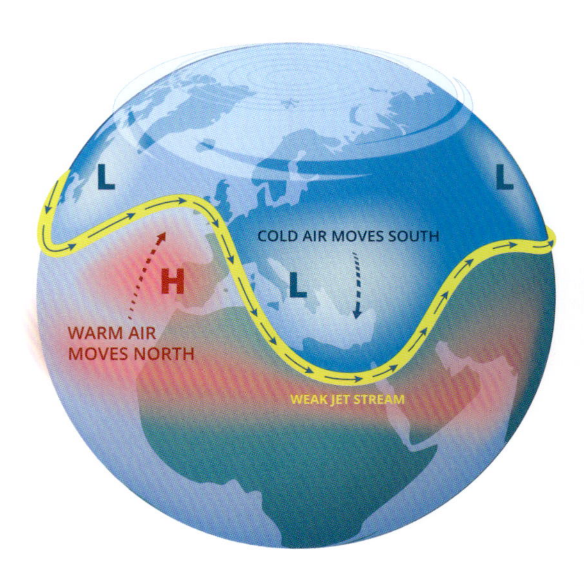

The path of a normal jet stream (left) is steady. When it's interrupted, the path changes course (right).

People can cause droughts. In some places, extra rainwater is saved for later. If people use too much water during a normal rainy season, there won't be enough water left when there isn't enough rain. People can also make droughts worse for others, often without meaning to. Some people get their water from a nearby river. If a drought is happening somewhere upriver from them, it will affect their supply of water.

People need rainwater to grow their garden plants and crops.

Drought caused this creek to dry up in the Sierra Nevada mountain range.

Droughts can begin a long time before anyone realizes it. Meteorologists measure rain and snow every day. Their computers compare these measurements to past measurements. If less and less rain or snow falls, there may be a drought. Other natural disasters, such as hurricanes or tornadoes, have a clear beginning and end. Droughts are called a creeping hazard of nature. That is because they start and end very slowly.

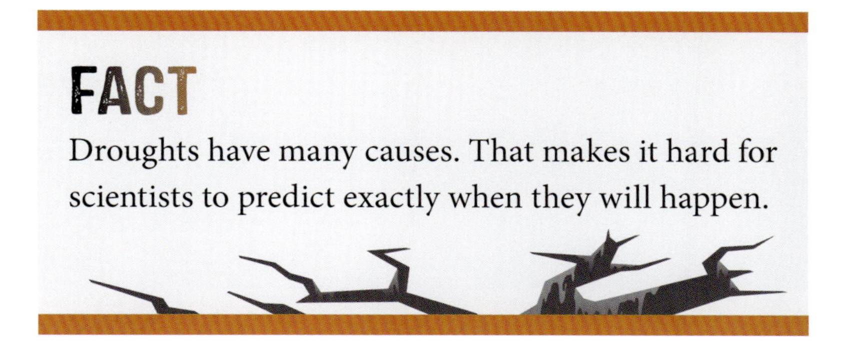

FACT

Droughts have many causes. That makes it hard for scientists to predict exactly when they will happen.

Chapter Two

DRY, CRACKED SOIL

Changes to the land are the first thing that happens because of a drought. The amount of moisture in the soil decreases. This can leave the ground so dry that cracks appear. Dry soil may even blow away because the plants that usually hold it in place die.

Hot, dry conditions can kill crops.

Drought means less **precipitation** of all kinds. Less snow falls in the winter. The mountains will have less **snowpack**. This means less snow melts in the spring to fill rivers, streams, and reservoirs.

Snow usually collects on mountains in the winter. When it melts, it runs downhill and makes bodies of water bigger.

Case Study

The Dust Bowl

One of the worst droughts in American history was the Dust Bowl of the 1930s. There was a drought in 80 percent of the country. Extremely strong winds on the Great Plains lifted dry soil into the air. The soil became clouds of dust and sand. These clouds blocked the sun for days at a time and made people sick. Thousands of children and people with breathing problems died. Many families were forced to leave their homes.

People helped the land recover by planting trees. The trees helped protect the land from strong winds. They also farmed differently, trying to protect the soil and finding new ways to water crops. By 1941, rainfall was back to normal levels.

What happens as a drought continues? The supply of water decreases. Many plants stop growing or turn brown to save water. Some drop their leaves. Farms produce fewer crops. Farmers may need to **irrigate** their crops. Because there are so many dried plants, grasses, and trees, the risk of wildfires is higher.

Chapter Three

WHAT HAPPENS TO ANIMALS

Droughts are not only hard for plants. Animals suffer too. When plants die, animals have less food to eat. Female animals may not be able to produce enough milk to feed their young. Animals such as bears and deer may find food in people's gardens or on farms. This can lead to conflict with humans.

In a drought, deer may look for food and water in people's yards.

Case Study

East Africa, 2024

Southern and eastern African countries experienced a long drought in 2024. Millions of people were unable to grow crops. Cattle and goats died because there was not enough water. Countries in these areas had gotten less than half of the rain they usually get. There was so little food that people were starving. Many had to leave their homes to survive. International aid organizations took donations from around the world to help. The groups brought food and clean water to affected areas.

Animals also may lose their **habitats**. Grasses, trees, and bushes die. These plants shelter many animals. Losing their shelter makes animals more **vulnerable**. Beavers, muskrats, and water birds may find their habitat shrinking. They are forced to live in smaller areas. They have to compete with other animals for space and food. Wetland areas where fish live or lay eggs can dry up. Fresh water dries up. Places where salt and fresh water meet might become too salty for fish to live there.

Muskrats live in swamps, marshes, and streams.

Birds and alligators gather at one of the only ponds left near Punta Gorda, Florida, during a 2022 drought.

Animals can still suffer after a drought is over. Habitats take time to regrow. There might be less land for grazing. Some animals may be weak because they haven't had enough to eat. Animals that don't have enough food or water may die. Animal populations may go down. Some species might even die out.

Chapter Four

AFTER A DROUGHT

Most droughts do end. But this can take a few months or many years. California had a severe drought that started in 2020. It did not end until 2023 after heavy snow fell on parts of the state. Some droughts start to end when it finally begins to rain. But one rainstorm won't end a drought. It takes many long, soaking rains to end droughts. Ground that is too dry can't absorb water. It flows off instead of soaking in. And if the rain comes too fast and strong, it can wash away the soil or cause flooding.

California saw record snowfalls in March 2023, after years of drought.

FACT

It can take as much as 15 inches (38 centimeters) of soaking rain to end a very severe drought.

Rain lands on dry, cracked soil.

The environment will not recover quickly. Some places never recover from long droughts. The soil may become too dry for rain to soak in. Even when it rains again, the area may become a desert. This is called desertification. Forests may not fully recover from droughts. Only some will go back to the way they were. Trees might be replaced by shrubs and grass. Some might be replaced by other species that need less water. Plants may never return to a healthy condition.

Evergreen trees that used to be in the huge boreal forest in Alaska are gone because of drought and fires. Shrubs and grasses have taken over. The trees may never return.

Dry conditions and erosion have turned a Ukrainian forest into a sandy desert.

A dry swamp bed in Barcelona, Spain

Animals are affected by a drought even after it ends. They may be weakened from lack of food. Some may have starved or died from disease, leaving fewer animals. Adult animals might have fewer **offspring**. Populations will then be smaller. Farm animals such as cattle may have less grass for grazing. They may be less healthy. The number of giraffes in Africa has gone down by 40 percent because of drought there. They do not have enough food or water.

Cattle in Illinois find water during a 2012 drought. The pasture where they usually grazed dried out.

During a drought, animals in Africa such as giraffes have to travel farther to find water sources.

Chapter Five

HUMANS AND DROUGHT

Droughts affect people as well as the environment. Some places have restrictions on how much water people can use. These restrictions might last long after rain begins falling again. This is because it takes a long time for the groundwater and the reservoirs to refill. People may also pay higher prices for food because farmers were not able to produce enough crops.

A water usage sign in New Zealand tells people what the current guidelines are.

FACT

Since 1900, drought has affected more than 2 billion people around the world. In the same amount of time, more than 11 million people have died because of drought.

Villagers in India gather water from the local well.

Some people still suffer after a drought. They may have lost family members to starvation. Some people become refugees. They move to other areas to find food and water.

Somali refugees collect water at a refugee camp in Kenya.

A dried-up riverbed on a farm in Walgett, Australia

Droughts are happening more often because of climate change. When the atmosphere warms by only 1.8 degrees Fahrenheit (1 degree Celsius), more droughts happen. Warmer temperatures make water evaporate faster. The air dries out when there is less moisture. It then pulls more moisture from the ground. This makes the soil dry out more quickly. Warmer winters mean less snow melts to fill streams and lakes.

Droughts will always happen. What can people do to be prepared? Farmers can use **sustainable** farming methods. This can limit how much groundwater they use for crops. Everyone can use less water at home. There will not be enough water for everyone on the planet unless we all work together to conserve water in our everyday lives.

Groups all over the world are working to reduce climate change. They teach people how to fight climate change in their own communities. People can also tell their government representatives to support issues that help limit climate change. Many aid groups help people who are suffering because of droughts. They need volunteers. Everyone can find a way to help build the future!

Case Study

The Tinderbox Drought

Southeast Australia had its worst drought in its history from 2017 to 2019. Only half of the usual amount of rain fell. The city of Sydney almost ran out of water. Farmers lost crops and animals. Australia had terrible forest fires in 2019 and 2020 because of the drought. The fires burned more than 22,000 square miles (56,980 square kilometers) of land. This event became known as the Tinderbox Drought. It ended in February 2020, when it began to rain. But it was April before the soil was as wet as usual. To get through the drought, people had to conserve water. This inspired new methods of water conservation.

Glossary

atmosphere (AT-muhs-feer)—the mixture of gases around a planet

current (KUH-rent)—the movement of water or air in a certain direction

evaporate (e-VAP-or-ate)—the process of liquid turning into a gas or vapor

habitat (HAB-i-tat)—the place where a plant or animal usually lives and grows

irrigate (ear-i-GATE)—to supply water to land or crops

jet stream (JET STREEM)—a band of air currents that circle the globe

offspring (OFF-spring)—the young of people or animals

precipitation (pri-sip-i-TAY-shuhn)—water falling from the sky as rain, snow, hail, or sleet

reservoir (REZ–uh–vore)—a natural or human-made place where water is collected and stored

snowpack (SNO-pak)—snow that has fallen on the ground and does not melt for months

sustainable (sus-TANE-i-bul)—using natural resources in a way that can be done again and for a long time

vulnerable (VUL-ner-i-bul)—able to be easily hurt or attacked

Read More

Murray, Julie. *Droughts*. Edina, MN: Abdo Zoom, 2024.

Schaefer, Lola. *Dangerous Droughts*. Minneapolis: Lerner Publications, 2022.

Tomecek, Steve. *All About Heat Waves and Droughts*. New York: Children's Press, 2022.

Internet Sites

Climate Kids: How Do We Know if We're in a Drought?
climatekids.nasa.gov/soil

National Drought Mitigation Center: Drought for Kids
drought.unl.edu/Education/DroughtforKids.aspx

National Geographic Education: Droughts 101
education.nationalgeographic.org/resource/droughts

Index

Africa, 15, 22
animals, 6, 14, 16, 17, 22, 29
atmosphere, 7, 27
Australia, 27, 29

California, 4, 5, 18
climate change, 27, 28
crops, 8, 10, 12, 13, 15, 24, 28, 29

desertification, 20
Dust Bowl, 12

erosion, 20

forest fires, 4, 29

habitats, 16, 17

jet stream, 7

megadroughts, 5
meteorologists, 9

snow, 6, 9, 11, 18, 27

Tinderbox Drought, 29

water cycle, 7

About the Author

Marcia Amidon Lusted has written 200 books and more than 600 articles for young readers of all ages. She is the former editor of *AppleSeeds* magazine for children. She also writes and edits for adults, as well as working in sustainable development. You can see more about her books at www.adventuresinnonfiction.com.